Varietals of Love

Your beautiful aroma
Carries hints of your love
And warm desire.

I gently touch
And hold
Your smooth glass
As I bring you
To me.

You touch my lips
As I taste you
And you envelop
My palate.

You are
The perfectly bodied wine.

Your tender tannins
And exquisite notes
Make me crave
Another bottle.

You caress my dreams
Softly
Like you used to
When you caressed
Your body
On mine.

Your perfumed presence
In the depths of my mind
Calms my soul.

The brightness
Of your lost smile
Wraps around me
Like your arms once did.

I long
To paint the canvas
Of your lips
With mine
Once again.

Bathing
In your warm rivers;

Walking
Among the flowers
Of your fields;

Touching
The soft earth
Of your rolling hills;

This is my Garden of Eden.

The peaks
Of the Ancient Pyramids
Do not compare
To the monuments
You erect.

The Hanging Gardens
Of Babylon
Do not compare
To the comfort
Of your oasis.

The Colossus of Rhodes
Does not compare
To the grandeur
Of your presence.

The Lighthouse
Of Alexandria
Does not compare
To the welcoming waters
Of your harbor.

The Temple
Of Artemis
Does not compare
To the warmth
Of your chambers.

The Statue of Zeus
Does not compare
To the thunderous feeling
Of your tender touch.

The Mausoleum
At Halicarnassus
Does not compare
To the desire
To die
In your arms.

To live without you
Is life without water
On a hot day.

To live without you
Is life without food
After a long fast.

To live without you
Is life without shelter
On a cold, rainy night.

To live without you
Is life without flowers
On a spring afternoon.

To live without you
Is life without life.

Deafness,
Blindness;

Muteness,
Dumbness;

Limbless,
Immobile;

Bedridden,
Terminal;

With overwhelming joy
Would I choose these
For but one more second
With you.

As we embraced
In total ecstasy,
Continents trembled
And came together.

Our souls cried out
To the heavens
With utmost joy
As we witnessed
Galaxies collide.

We felt
The pulse
Of the Earth,
And the warmth
Of entire suns.

You and I,
Along with all of life,
Became one.

The instrument
Of your voice
And the symphony
Of your skin
Is God's
Most wonderful
Composition.

With you
I was the richest man
In the world.

With you
I had everything
I needed.

Without you
My soul
Is impoverished.

Without you
I have lost
All the treasures
I could ever need.

The sound
And the beat
Of our percussion
Echoes
Throughout.

The music
Of generations
Continues
With our movements.

Operatic cries
Carry
Through the night.

We are unknown royalty;
Let no one sleep!

You were my Queen,
Meant to bear
The heirs
To our kingdom.

Now my kingdom lay bare.

I have been stripped
Of all titles;
My authority
Is none.

The burning foundations
Surround me,
I hold you,
Lifeless and unspeaking.

Could I explore
Your oceans
Once more?

The life
They contained
Encased me
In happiness.

As I went under,
They nourished me.

On this dry land
I thirst;
For them
And for you.

O to hear
The gentle beat
Of your heart
As we come closer.

O to feel
The subtle sweat
Of your back
As we both dance.

O to feel
Your hushed breath
Touch me
As my skin shivers
In anticipation.

Gazing
Into your eyes,
Allowing me
To look back in time
At your joys
And your pains,
Was a privilege
Any man
Would treasure to have.

I despair
At having nothing
To look back in time
To gaze
Into the precious pearls
That are your eyes
Once more.

By the fire;
Under the moonlight;
Among the stars;

By running waters;
Under the sunlight;
Among the mountains;

These were the stages
Upon which
We embraced
And kissed.

Why
Can I no longer find
The home we built,
You and I?

It stood strong;
The warmth
It exuded
Was unparalleled.

How
Could it disappear
So suddenly?

I will keep looking
Until I find it
And you
Again.

I want to sit
At the winery
Of your kiss.

I want to eat
At the restaurant
Of your touch.

I want to drink
At the brewery
Of your love.

I want sleep
In the resort
Of your intimacy.

I wake up
From the dream
Of our marriage
Of our family
Of our children
Of growing old
With you.

It was only
A dream
Which makes my life
A nightmare.

You were
The cure
To my disease.

You were
The quenching
Of my thirst.

Now
I lay dying;
With my last breath,
I only
Think of you.

Who will comfort me
When I cry?

Who will laugh with me
When I laugh?

Who will kiss me
When I need love?

Who will grow old with me
As I grow old?

In the library of life,
You were the one book
I wanted to read
For the rest of mine.

Here I stand
At your grave,
Trying to keep
The flowers I lay there
Alive.

But my prayers
Do not reach
Your angelic ears.

Now is the time
I let go
Of your grip.

Now is the time
I let you
Fade away.

Only then
Will I heal.